clash

POETRY

clash

POETRY

SAD SEXY CATHOLIC

LAUREN BADILLO MILICI

Sad Sexy Catholic is the girl at the rock show, the one who exudes effortless cool in vintage leather and ripped tights. But when you turn to talk to her, she's gone. In this haunting collection, Lauren Badillo Milici offers anthems for the heartbreakers as well as the heartbroken. This is a catalogue of precautionary tales and premonitions that stretches from abject darkness to "the pink light of dawn." Unflinchingly, the speaker walks us through lonely halls with "an emptiness like winter." A hereditary witch, she's jaded enough to tell the hardest truths but tender enough to call out to us: "if you're going to scream, scream with me." Step inside, lost girls. You're home.

— Rita Mookerjee, author of *False Offering* (Jackleg Press 2023)

In **Sad Sexy Catholic**, Lauren Badillo Milici gives us a leading lady with a storyline of multiple twists, turns, and most importantly, reclamations. The camera is focused on her, and she twists its patriarchal lens with a feminism that questions what is truly holy. This collection purrs, then takes its claws out. She gives us pure tenderness, and Dear, she guards that with her heart. Milici's speaker is all diamond—they're the femme fatale who writes their own ending to the story—it's everlasting, like a tattoo of lip prints.

5

— Dorothy Chan, author of *Babe* (Diode Editions) and *Attack of the Fifty-Foot Centerfold* (Spork Press)

6

SAD SEXY CATHOLIC

INDEX

8

9

"The heart is deceitful above all things, and desperately wicked: who can know it?"

— Jeremiah 17:9

"A young woman will drive you places you never meant to go."

— Patrick Stump, "Everybody Wants Somebody"

for the sinners

13

14

EVE WAS FRAMED

Today, a boy says, *good news: I love you again,*

as if this were a gift. As if all men were God.

Instead, church bells. A forgotten hymn

from the Book of Revelation—

something that hurts

in a way John could never find a name for.

Luckily, the past is never dead. It's not even past.

In a memory, the surgeon hands me a warm bag

of my own blood.

Say this aloud. It will not protect you.

BOUND

think of all the ways you want

> but can't have

>> how one drunken October you told me

> you'd like to try it sometime

how does it feel?

>> darling it's like kneeling in gold

> like giving yourself over to God

when you ask me how I'm doing I want to tell you

> that I sent a photo of my body to a stranger

>> that I bite

> but I've never bitten

>>>> you

18

MY BOYFRIEND WANTS TO DIE

by steering a yacht   straight
into the eye   of a storm.
He tells me this over coffee
or in bed.   Once, he jumped
in front of a moving car.
Once, he woke up in a field
not far from where Hank Williams
stopped   his   own   heart.
My boyfriend doesn't believe
in *after*. There is only *now*
and *then*. That's fine. We hike
to the highest point & hold
each other—initials of old lovers
carved into the rocks beneath
us.   In the stillness, I listen
for the *ba-dum-thunk-thunk*
of his irregular hearbeat. *We live
over there, by the smokestacks.*
He points north, to the river
but I am staring   at his finger,
wanting to put it in my pocket,
keep it safe   from everything.

REMEMBER WHEN I CRIED IN THAT CHURCH WE FOUND?

why ask
if you already know

the answer, lauren / birds fly
out of my mouth

all the goddamn time
the woman i love

is too sad / to breathe
hi sweetheart hi

darling anywhere i am is lonely so
don't take it personally

IT ONLY TOOK A WHISPER

I leave because I'm good
at that —there's always some bullshit
reason to kill your girlfriend. A ghost
is a ghost is a ghost. Consider:
bloodletting as therapy or, *wrists are for girls,*
I'm slitting my own throat. Night
becomes morning becomes a bluer shade of dark
& nothing matters. Not even you.

AN ADMISSION OF SOMETHING
OTHER THAN GUILT

Before us, an emptiness like winter.

The tongue cut   and replaced.

Can you see me out there by the flowers?

Sometimes, my arms bend back.

Not the skin pulled taut but split   at the knuckle.

My face, shaped like a strange diamond.

I am not. Here. I am.

I won't take anything off for you.

on the last cold night of March I fall
asleep in my clothes & dream of burial-
--every acre of my lover's farm turned
over with shovels meant only for the
smallest garden. in the morning, I think
about making him swear. *cut your palm
open and press it against mine. there.* I write
my own ending to the story about the
missing woman who left her car in the
middle of an Amherst road, tell her
mother she changed her name & settled
down. my lover is missing almost all
of the time because *hell is other people*
& I don't want to worry about the soil
anymore, but I will.

27

YOUR EX-GIRLFRIEND COMES TO
ME IN A DREAM AND REMINDS
ME THAT I AIN'T SHIT

No, darlin',
we *all* want the fairytale:
each of us done up & dressed
in our Sunday's best
because we just can't wait
to meet his momma.
Do you feel held by him?
Yeah, us too. You're not the only one
who thinks his voice sounds
like summer / or that his eyes are so fucking blue
you could drown in them / or whatever cliché
bullshit you purred into the phone
at four in the morning because you like
that he makes you lose sleep.
There's nothing diamond about you;
nothing pretty you could say
to make him pick you first.
He's perfect—
made of the same plastic
that makes Ken dolls melt in the sun
leaving all the Barbies
to wonder.

30

THE COURT ORDERS THERAPY
AFTER THE HOUSE FIRE

when the Nice Lady
gives you
the doll
& says
show me
what you want
to do
you hold it
in your small hands

IN CASE YOU WERE WONDERING

I love a girl who can dance to anything.

If you're gonna scream, scream with me.

Nothing inside me feels wild.

The nicotine turning our fingers into ten yellow moons.

I held it under my tongue for as long as I could.

Thanks, sorry, sure.

Only I know the pink light of dawn.

In the morning, I will become something else entirely.

MEDITATION

These days, I am grateful for consistency—

How my lover reaches for me in the dead of night,
panicked, soft hand on my stomach.

Or the way a diamond dove coos from the top
of its cage; sweet, gentle mourning of nothing.

The truth is: I can no longer handle loss
of any kind.

I need the small, careful stars painted
on the stairs to his apartment, the echo
of my heels on every single step.

I need the stomachache that feels like bird beaks
and teeth, the anxiety that comes with starting.

I need I need I need.

Tonight, I mistake the moon for a streetlight.

I forget how to soften, how it feels to have faith
in anything.

FIVE OF WANDS

I want a gentle war.

Send your best men
out to sea.

A heavy body will float
in saltwater,
will float better
if dead.

I want a quiet hymn.

The way doves
are not songbirds,
but symbols
of grief.

There is new blood
in the soil,
rain, a serum
for growth.

The Moon wants me
to open the blinds
when I make love,
but I won't.

SAD SEXY CATHOLIC

I was God's favorite, once—enough
schoolgirl in me to make Mary
sweat. not a fall-from-grace,
but something sweeter. an unlit cigarette
wedged between two adolescent fingers;
& the skin like bruised fruit. now,
the only notion of *holy*   pressed
between opaque pages, or bound
at the wrists. The sacrament of confession,
or the first time I ran my tongue
along someone else's teeth. Enough
obedience in me to serve man,
to kneel in velvet & say a little prayer
for every single bead
of sweat.

WHEN JAMES ENTERS THE HOUSE IN BLAIR WITCH (2016)

the door locks behind him, obviously—
haven't you ever seen a scary movie?
this is the one / where the monster
is grief. nobody fucks
not even in the pitch black
lullabied by the *scratchscratchscratch*
of branches like fingers like *Heather,*
is that you?
when the door locks, everyone dies
but you already knew that:
the Final Girl follows James / the camera
cuts out   cuts back   static   static   static
& suddenly, blood
suddenly, the long-limbed flesh
of something faceless
& James, you did this:
split the tree at the root / hung your friends
from the branches
you said: m*y sister is still out there*
as if she held her last breath
for you

ALL THE GOOD GIRLS GO MISSING

it's too hard so I stay
in for the night.

good, he says—girls like you
always go missing. don't

be so small & blonde.

but what if I like being bad

at this? ask where

he hit me and I'll let you.

44

THIS LOVE IS

a curse, yes. Sad, small enchantment.

When did we stop kissing? November?

I want rid of this,

I tell you over   and over.

A bare lightbulb in the bedroom,

and my bobby pins, everywhere. Purposeful.

The King of Wands said you would undo us,

but I ignored him, shuffled the card back into its deck.

I'm not sure about the order of things.

First, there was a fire. Then, we built a house.

Fail homeward, you said—

as if this were easy.

As if you always knew I was never   any good.

LISTENING TO THE JAMES BOND THEME ON THE WAY TO BOSTON LOGAN AIRPORT

It's not the worst winter I've ever felt
so I crack the window, remember
the harbor. Remember the drink
Emily fixed me—a Moonbeam,
gin, vodka, crème de violette.
In this cab, I smile at no one
but My Own Tired Reflection
bemoaning these ungodly hours
& longing for my queen bed
back at Cloud Place. My driver
mumbles to himself, says,
these city lights are inside of us,
but it seems fake. Still, the skyscrapers
sparkle in a way that makes me hate
New York. I let myself be romanced
by the violins, the radio anything
but silent, and, anyway, this feels
like the end of something.

ORACLE

I won't tell you
what I've done
to my body.

We can blame the ghosts
for the fingerprints,
the bruises above my knee.

Nothing ever happens
on purpose.
You know this.

How we tried to trick fate
with tarot cards, spells we poured
into the kitchen sink.

I predicted the parkway crash,
but couldn't tell you. This crystal ball,
my mother's. A gift I wasn't ready for.

I burn this sage
to keep the demons
from my bed.

They belong
to me
and only me.

AREN'T WE LUCKY

this is the good kind of cliché
where the boy is the only youngblondething
left in town & he's lonely
the way God was lonely
when He made fucking everything
even the front lawn in West Virginia
littered with cigarettes
like petals   thrown down the aisle
and he needs to be
the kid who comes
alive
& kisses the first girl he sees
as if his heart isn't already the shape
of a permanent fist
but *whatever you want, I'll be*
& *aren't we lucky?*
& isn't this the part in the movie
where the boy drunk-stumbles home / and says,
I'm sorry, mom
for everything

I WISH THE SOFT ANIMAL OF MY BODY WOULD SHUT THE FUCK UP

after Mary Oliver

meanwhile the men whose love i do not need
are free. the world goes on and on
and on. i can't tell you about despair
but there are thorns
where there shouldn't be—
the body doesn't always   want.
when the heat chokes what's left
of spring, god will send a flood.
don't repent. do not ask
for a miracle. whoever you are,
harsh and lonely, is headed home
again. wait for the fireflies—
a soft glow, a swarm.
you do not have
to be good.
don't.

DAYLIGHT

today I am grateful for the spiders
on my balcony, the citrus that keeps
the kittens from tearing up the velvet.

everything is precious, even the bathwater
discarded lily stems, dried lavender
stuck to the carpet.

the therapist says to savor this,
as if it's the only goodness left
in West Virginia.

as if this is the only goodness
that I will ever get.

THE ONLY THING LEFT TO DO IN THIS TOWN IS MAKE A MESS AND THEN LEAVE

so
I throw myself
into bed with a boy
who's too young to know
how the body will die
if it can't find a way
to empty.

THE POEM COMES QUICK

like you—
a soft
unraveling
followed
by
silence.

I THINK BURT REYNOLDS IS THE KIND OF GUY WHO KEEPS THE LIGHTS ON

tonight the sky is purple-yellow fire
& I've spent the day in bed.
sometimes I want a motel scene
starring coke on the dresser
or a gun in my hand.
I want the fairytale.
once I was drunk in the back of a cab
& a song came on the radio
that made me miss my mother.
I'm not too good at this anymore.
sometimes when a man says
I want to pin you
he means, to the wall
mounted like a prized buck.
we can talk about anything you want,
as long as you're naked.
well I'm not,
but I could be.

BRIGHT WHITE LIGHT
for Henry Zebrowski

This week, the psychic is on vacation.
glow glow glow and then nothing—
as if something came through and killed
all the fireflies.
In the bible, it's the woman who looks back—
born of man; cunt crafted from ribcage.
It wasn't always like this.
When the bridge collapsed,
no one blamed God.
It's better with a gun in your face.
If I knew the truth, I wouldn't tell you anyway.

SOMETIMES MY ARMS BEND BACK

Oh Donna, the dead talk to me
all the time. When I forget to be good,
they whisper. All I wanted was a motel
scene starring coke on the dresser
or a gun in my hand. I wanted the fairytale.
Tonight, I bloom in reverse — the buds tightening
like fists. Over drinks, I say *die*. I say *leave me* and *don't*.
When they ask what happened, tell them a witch
pricked my finger. Tell them I washed up on shore.

LOVE POEM IN SPITE OF EVERYTHING

after Emily O'Neill

for Ash

I love you cherrytomatopepperbasil I love you
coffeehouse Saturday / cream & sugar I love you
broken grocery bag / overwatered philodendron

the hoya carnosa clippings kept alive
in a milk glass / I love you too many streetlights
to see the stars from our front yard

but baby we can build a fire / and the neighbors
gather 'round / I love you boba tea latte
pork carnitas / bouquet of blue hydrangea

I love you half-moon empanada I love you
snowstorm in West Virginia / holding hands
inside my sweater / monarch cicada summer

& the house we've built / the tenderness
that lives / in a terra cotta pot / thriving in spite
of everything

SORRU

the boy you wanted so bad
asks how wide your mouth can go

so you show him—
wider, the boy says. *suffer,*

so you do. your body,
an offering. your breasts,

a novena. *don't leave,*
but he does. lay in wait

like a proper saint. don't forget
to be good.

WHAT I AM ABOUT TO DO HAS NOT BEEN APPROVED BY THE VATICAN

I softened for you, raggedy
boy.
Your unmade bed. Your body,
an omen. I knew better.
I won't

go gently, no—
You knew
this would end
in a knife
fight. An exchanging
of teeth.

I place your name
in my
mouth
& spit
the letters
into sigils.

This is the part where I show you
how good I am
at
everything.
Even this.

NOTES

The title, "I Think Burt Reynolds Is the Kind of Guy Who Leaves the Lights On" is borrowed from the play, *Stripped* by Tyler Grimes.

The title, "What I Am About to Do Has Not Been Approved by The Vatican" is taken from the PC horror game, *Faith* by Airdorf Games.

The title "Sometimes My Arms Bend Back," is borrowed from the TV show, *Twin Peaks*.

The poem, "Love Poem in Spite of Everything," is based on the poem, "Love is a Weakness" by Emily O'Neill from the book, *A Falling Knife Has No Handle*.

The line, "The stomachache that feels like bird beaks and teeth," is borrowed from the book, *The Boy with the Thorn in His Side* by Pete Wentz.

ACKNOWLEDGEMENTS

Thanks to the editors of the following publications in which these poems appeared, sometimes in slightly different forms:

BEST BUDS! A Collective: "Bright White Light; My Boyfriend Wants to Die; Meditation on Healing"

Cloves Literary: "I Wish the Soft Animal of My Body Would Shut the Fuck Up"

Epiphany: A Literary Journal: "Meditation"

HaveHasHad: "I Think Burt Reynolds is the Kind of Guy Who Keeps the Lights On"

Hobart: "Sad Sexy Catholic"

jubilat: Eve Was Framed

Wax Nine: "When James Goes Into the House In Blair Witch (2016); Remember When I Cried in That Church We Found?; It Only Took A Whisper"

Special thanks to my sister Gianna / my parents The Bob & Ivette / my honorary sisters Sam Bloom and Heather Myers / my chosen familia Tory, Ely, & Bella / my actual wife Alicia / the endlessly inspiring and enormously talented Kris Straub / rainbow person Paige Lacoste / cat-sitter & life-saver extraordinaire Annuh Bailey / earth angels Addison & Kacey / Sweet Dorothy + Lovely Rita / sweetheart Mel Grigsby / Kolleen Carney Hoepfner, Danielle Sinay, and Elle Nash aka the big sisters I never had / cat-bringer Ash Orr / beauty cuties Payton O. & Payton P / Mark Randles, Ryan Larson, Brandon, Brendan H., Kyle Mares, The Mike, & Peter S. <3 / Henry Zebrowski for being the kindest and weirdest person I've ever met / everyone who has ever supported me via Patreon I love you all so much / and of course, Leza & Christoph for taking a chance on a tiny sexy chapbook

Dedicated to the memory of Brian Cho. I know you would've loved these poems and I'll never ever stop missing you.

LAUREN BADILLO MILICI

Lauren Badillo Milici is a cat mom first and raging bitch second. Her hobbies include swearing, kissing strange men at bars, and eating donuts while lying down. She has an MFA in Poetry but refuses to talk about it. Malcolm McDowell called her 'lovely' at a convention once.

ALSO BY CLASH BOOKS

GAG REFLEX
Elle Nash

WHAT ARE YOU
Lindsay Lerman

PSYCHROS
Charlene Elsby

AT SEA
Aïcha Martine Thiam

THE SMALLEST OF BONES
Holly Lyn Walrath

AN EXHALATION OF DEAD THINGS
Savannah Slone

WATERFALL GIRLS
Kimberly White

ALL THE PLACES I WISH I DIED
Crystal Stone

LIFE OF THE PARTY
Tea Hacic-Vlahovic

GIRL LIKE A BOMB
Autumn Christian

THE ELVIS MACHINE
Kim Vodicka

WE PUT THE LIT IN LITERARY
clashbooks.com

 @clashbooks @clashbooks /clashbooks

Email
clashmediabooks@gmail.com